SPECTRUM®
READERS

LEVEL 3

EPIC!
Statues and Monuments

By Teresa Domnauer

 Carson-Dellosa
Publishing

SPECTRUM®

An imprint of Carson-Dellosa Publishing, LLC
P.O. Box 35665
Greensboro, NC 27425-5665

carsondellosa.com

Printed in the USA. All rights reserved.
ISBN 978-1-4838-0128-5

01-002141120

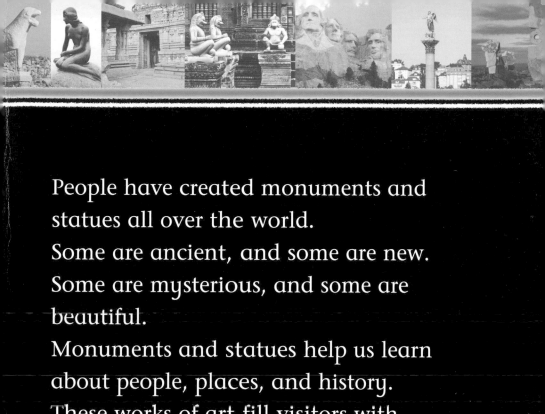

People have created monuments and statues all over the world.
Some are ancient, and some are new.
Some are mysterious, and some are beautiful.
Monuments and statues help us learn about people, places, and history.
These works of art fill visitors with wonder and awe.

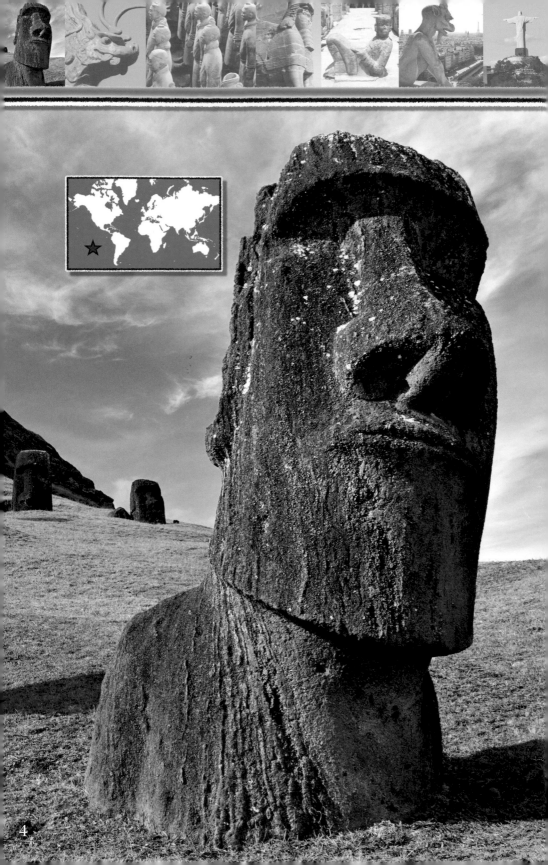

The Massive Moai

Far out in the Pacific Ocean is Easter Island, the world's most isolated inhabited island.

Here, you can see the mysterious Moai (MOH eye) statues.

No one knows why they were built. Ancient people carved hundreds of them from volcanic rock.

Archaeologists do not know how people moved the statues around the island without machines or wheels.

Fascinating Facts

- Archaeologists believe the Moai statues are over 400 years old.
- The largest statue is 37 feet high—that's taller than a house!

The Forbidden City

If you visit Beijing, China, you can see the Forbidden City.
The walled city contains over 900 buildings, all decorated with statues.
The powerful Chinese emperor Yongle began building the city in 1406.
It took over 14 years to build.
Fierce dragon statues along the rooftops help protect the city.

Fascinating Facts

- No one except the emperor could travel freely in the Forbidden City without permission.

- Today, the Forbidden City is a museum, and millions of tourists visit each year.

Terra Cotta Army

In 1974, some farmers made an incredible discovery while digging wells.

They found a life-size statue of an ancient soldier made from clay.

Archaeologists were immediately called to the site near Xi'an, China.

They unearthed 8,000 clay soldiers!

The soldiers were made for the first emperor, or ruler, of China.

They stood in rows like a real army to protect the emperor's burial place.

Fascinating Facts

- An entire museum in China is built around the Terra Cotta Army.

- Over 700,000 workers created the army, which had been buried for over 2,000 years.

9

Winged Bulls

Magnificent winged bulls watch over the ruins of the ancient capital Persepolis (purr SEP uh liss).

Ruins are parts of ancient buildings that are still standing.

Each statue has the head of a king, the wings of an eagle, and the body of a powerful bull.

The bulls stand on columns built by ancient Persian rulers.

Fascinating Facts

- The buildings and statues at Persepolis were built about 2,500 years ago.
- Today, Persia is the country of Iran.

Mysteries in Mexico

The ancient city Chichén Itzá (CHEE chen EET zah) holds many treasures.

Here, you will find a kind of statue called a *chac mool*.

These sculptures were created before Spanish explorers came to Mexico and show human figures lying back with knees together.

Archaeologists are not sure what they represent.

They may be great warriors.

Fascinating Facts

- The Mayan people originally inhabited this part of Mexico.

- Over three dozen chac mool statues have been found at Chichén Itzá.

14

Grotesque Gargoyles

In Paris, France, you can see gargoyles high atop Notre Dame Cathedral.

This enormous church was built beginning in the year 1163.

Gargoyles on the roof of the cathedral look as though they are half man, half beast. These spooky creatures have a special job. When it rains, water flows over them and away from the building.

Fascinating Facts

- It took over 100 years to complete Notre Dame!

- The cathedral is full of art—from stone sculptures, to paintings, to stained glass.

Mountaintop Monument

The enormous statue *Christ the Redeemer* stands on a mountain high above the city of Rio de Janeiro, Brazil.

It is 98 feet tall—nearly as tall as a ten-story building!

The arms of the monument stretch almost as wide as its height.

Completed in 1931, the concrete statue is covered in small triangular tiles.

Fascinating Facts

- In 1922, a contest was held to find a designer for the statue. The winner was Heitor da Silva Costa.

- During construction, workers were transported up the mountain by railway.

Terrace of the Lions

In ancient times, to reach a temple on the island of Delos, Greece, you had to pass by lions!

Originally, nine fierce marble lions lined the path on the Terrace of the Lions. Today, copies stand in their place.

The ancient Greeks held festivals on Delos with music, dance, and athletic contests. The ruins at Delos are over 2,600 years old, and very little remains of them.

Fascinating Facts

- Five of the original lions are kept safely in museums.
- The ancient Greeks believed that Delos was the birthplace of the Greek god Apollo.

19

The Little Mermaid

If you visit the city of Copenhagen, Denmark, you can see the statue *The Little Mermaid*.

You might already know the tale of "The Little Mermaid," written by Hans Christian Andersen.

Danish sculptor Edvard Eriksen made the bronze statue in 1913.

It is beloved by the people of Denmark. Thousands of tourists take photos with the mermaid each year.

Fascinating Facts

- There are copies of *The Little Mermaid* statue all around the world.
- The sculptor's wife modeled for the statue.

Krishna Temple

Krishna Temple in Hampi, India, is a special place of worship.
A king built it nearly five hundred years ago, but it still stands in good condition. Its huge entrance has sculptures of elephants and carvings that tell stories. Once, a road designed for chariots led to the temple door.
A stone container stood ready to receive offerings of grain.

Fascinating Facts

- Visitors to Krishna Temple can climb stairs to the top for an amazing view.
- Banana plantations can be found near the temple.

Fortress of Beauty

A Hindu temple near Angkor, Cambodia, is much smaller than the Krishna Temple. A royal counselor built it from deep red sandstone over a thousand years ago. Visitors admire fine carvings and sculptures that decorate every surface. Many show scenes from ancient stories. The temple's name, Banteay Srei, means "fortress of beauty."

Fascinating Facts

- In 1923, four sculptures were stolen from the temple. They were quickly returned when the thief was caught.

- In 1930, the temple was taken apart piece by piece and put back together!

An American Monument

Mt. Rushmore emerges from a cliff in the Black Hills of South Dakota.

The faces of U.S. presidents George Washington, Thomas Jefferson, Abraham Lincoln, and Theodore Roosevelt stare out proudly from the rocks.

The massive monument represents the first 150 years of United States history.

Fascinating Facts

- The construction of Mt. Rushmore began in 1927 and took 14 years to complete.
- Most of Mt. Rushmore was carved by blasting dynamite to remove tons of rock.

Jubilee Column

The King William Jubilee Column forms the center of Palace Square in Stuttgart, Germany.

The winged goddess Concordia perches on top of the column.

The New Palace stands behind it.

In the past, the square was used for military practice.

Today, people enjoy holiday markets, festivals, and concerts in the square.

Fascinating Facts

- The statue of Concordia symbolizes harmony and peace.
- The Jubilee Column was built in 1841.

Statues in the Outback

The remote deserts of Australia are known as the *Outback*.

There, in Living Desert State Park, you can see the Living Desert Sculptures.

The park can be found near Broken Hill in New South Wales, Australia.

Artists from around the world created the interesting sandstone sculptures in 1993.

Fascinating Facts

- As you walk along the park trail, you might see a kangaroo hop by.

- Broken Hill is known as Silver City because of its rich silver mines.

EPIC! Statues and Monuments Comprehension Questions

1. Which presidents are featured at Mt. Rushmore?

2. Where is the Terrace of the Lions?

3. Why do you think statues and monuments are important?

4. Where is Easter Island?

5. Where could you find chac mool statues?

6. Where can you find the Living Desert Sculptures?

7. What is the name of a famous statue in Copenhagen, Denmark?

8. How would you describe a gargoyle?

9. Which two monuments are Hindu temples?

10. Who discovered the Terra Cotta Army?

11. Where is the Forbidden City?

12. What is an ancient ruin?